"Now to him who is able to do exceedingly abundantly above all that we ask or think, according to the power that works in us..."

Ephesians 3:20

This scripture journey belongs to:

____

CONTENTS

HOW TO GET THE MOST OUT OF THIS JOURNEY

Each day's 10–15 minute devotion includes a verse-by-verse Scripture reading through the entire Book of Ephesians with reflection questions, a prayer prompt, and space to journal your thoughts. Whether you're new to devotionals or a seasoned believer, this unique approach offers you a way to grow closer to experiencing an abundant life in Christ through the authority of God's Word.

This Scripture Journey is perfect for personal quiet time, one-on-one discipleship, small groups, and/or family Bible night, complete with helpful discussion guides in the back.

Here are four simple habits to abide in Christ - and actually finish strong:

Start Small – Begin where you are - not where you think you should be. Read the day's Scripture or try just one of the reflection questions. Build spiritual habits gradually over the 30 days.

Set an Appointment – Choose a consistent time and place for your devotions, whether it's 10 minutes in the morning or a quiet evening moment. Be intentional.

Stay Steady – Showing up is the key to building up. Consistency is far more important than intensity. Miss a session? No problem. Pick up later that day or jump to the current day's reading.

Switch Things Up – Invite a friend or family member to join you occasionally. Discussing insights together and using the group guide reinforces your growth. There are two helpful guides at the end of this book: one for small group discussion and the other for a family Bible study.

No matter your schedule or experience, this 30-day journey through Ephesians fits into your life. If you're new to this type of devotional - no worries—each day's prompts are simple and clear. If you fall behind, just pick up where you left off. Repetition is the key to formation.

Imagine the peace of knowing Christ more deeply and facing life's challenges with joy. Start Day 1 today, and let this journey guide you to a stronger, more vibrant faith over the next 30 days. Don't wait, take the first step toward a closer walk with Jesus!

THE P.R.A.Y. METHOD

As a believer in Christ, you're invited to grow closer to God daily through His Word. **The P.R.A.Y. Method** - Pray, Read, Ask, Yield - is a simple, powerful way to connect with Jesus, especially when paired with this 30-day devotional journal, *Walking with Jesus through the Book of Ephesians*. Each P.R.A.Y. step takes about 10-15 minutes daily but can be adapted for busier days.

PRAY

Begin with prayer to center your heart on God, who is, "Our Father" (Matthew 6:9). Use the journal's daily prayer prompt, The Lord's Prayer, or just a simple heart-felt prayer like, "Lord, open my heart to Your Word today." Prayer sets the tone for your devotional time. Each day also includes prompts for "Listening Prayers" as well.

> *Tip:* Start small—try the journal's prayer prompt if you're new to praying.

READ

Reading Scripture daily helps us stay grounded and growing in the truth of God's Word. Each day in this devotional provides a short passage from the Apostle Paul's letter to the Ephesians. This letter was written to a young, growing body of believers in the heavily secularized city of Ephesus who needed strong foundational teaching. These teachings are very relevant for us today as well.

> *Tip:* Choose a consistent time and place, like 10-15 minutes each morning. If you're running late, try using a Bible app that reads the Scriptures to you while you're on the go.

ASK

Asking good questions based on what we've read opens us up to divinely inspired answers. Meditate on the day's passage by reflecting on the journal's discovery question or ask, "What does this passage help me discover about Jesus?" Journal your thoughts in the spaces.

> *Tip:* Try to think about 1 verse you read that morning throughout the day. Maybe write it on a sticky note and post it where you can look at it often.

YIELD

Yielding is giving God the right of way. When you are having a bad day – like when someone cuts you off in traffic - the Holy Spirit may nudge you to release anger and recall what you read in Scripture that day. For example, the Apostle Paul reminds us in Ephesians 4:2-3, …*"with all lowliness and humility, with patience, bearing with one another in love, being eager to keep the unity of the Spirit in the bond of peace."*

> *Tip:* Stay in tune or "in step" with the Holy Spirit throughout the day (Galatians 5:25). Ask the Lord to help you reflect on what you read that morning throughout the day.

Use this P.R.A.Y Method as you journey through Ephesians each day over the next 30 days to enhance your reading and deepen your ability to stay strong in your authority in Christ!

A RECOMMENDED PRACTICE

Our reception of God's truth is often determined by the posture of our heart. Jesus teaches a powerful principle about the Word of God in The Parable of the Sower. This parable is found in Matthew 13:1-23, Mark 4:1-20, and Luke 8:4-15. Jesus describes Himself as the Sower, the seed as God's Word, and the soil can be described as the condition of the human heart.

God's Word is the seed of His message to us! But, where there is a hardness of heart, the seed never penetrates the soil. It is snatched away, and the seed never gets the chance to bear the fruit that it was intended to produce. The "good soil", however, is a heart that is softened, humble, and ready to receive the seed.

As famous preacher Charles Spurgeon once said:

> *"Therefore, O heavenly Sower, plough me first,*
> *and then cast the truth into me, and let me yield to Thee*
> *a bounteous harvest."*

We encourage you to take a moment to pray a prayer before you dive into the daily readings so that your heart will be properly postured to receive the good seed of God's Word.

You may use The Lord's Prayer, the following "Posture Prayer," and/or feel free to create your own heartfelt prayer. Be convinced each day that God's Word is alive - as promised in Hebrews 4:12. And according to Isaiah 55:11, the Lord directs His Word to accomplish wonderful things in the lives of those whose hearts are prepared to receive it.

"POSTURE PRAYER"
A Prayer for Softening the Soil

Father - You are Holy, You are just, and You are true. Your Word is truth. You are Love. Thank You, Father, for loving me, for saving me, and for making me complete in Christ. Forgive me, Father, for believing any lies about You or for having any misunderstandings about Your Word.

Help my heart be like soft soil as I read Your Word today so I will understand it, receive it, and apply it to my life and to help others do so as well. In Jesus' name I pray, Amen.

EPHESIANS: AN OVERVIEW

Author: Apostle Paul

Date: Likely A.D. 60-62 (sometime after Paul's missionary journey to Ephesus in the early 50's).

Genre: Pauline Epistle. A letter written to encourage believers by the Apostle Paul. Some consider it to be a "circular letter" meant to be read to a wide area of believers in that region.

Setting: Imagine a huge city so steeped in idol worship, mysticism, and godless culture that its skyline was dominated with what was once considered one of the 7 Wonders of the World: The Temple of Artemis. Every day, thousands would flock to that temple to offer sacrifices, purchase silver idols and worship a cult that promised prosperity and power. Suddenly a missionary enters this pagan palladium armed with the truth of the Gospel of Jesus Christ: the Apostle Paul. According to Acts 18-20, Paul preached, ministered, and established churches in that great city for nearly 3 years. A decade later Paul would write them this letter – Ephesians – to encourage them and remind them of the victory and authority they have as believers in Christ. Over time, the old gods faded and the once great temple fell into ruin - eventually reduced to a single column. The once dominant secularism and idolatry of Ephesus was transformed by the light of the Gospel.

Purpose: Ephesians is considered one of Paul's "Prison Letters" (including Philippians, Colossians and Philemon) that he wrote while awaiting trial, imprisoned in Rome. Some of the reasons Paul wrote this letter of encouragement was to reassure them of Christ's superiority (Chapter 1), remind them of their inheritance in Christ (2), and to unveil the "mystery" of the unity of Messianic Jews and Christian Gentiles as one reconciled family in Christ (2:11-3:9). Additionally, Paul addresses the purpose of the Church (4), the importance of family (5) and the believer's authority (6). The letter is often categorized in two parts: The Believer's Position (1-3) and The Believer's Practice (4-6). This letter is as relevant and necessary to 21st century believers as it was to the 1st century believers.

Key Verse:

"Now to him who is able to do exceedingly abundantly above all that we ask or think, according to the power that works in us..." - Ephesians 3:20

Key Themes:

1. The Authority of Christ's Position (Ephesians 1:1-2:10)

2. The Authority of the Believer's Position (Ephesians 2:11-3:21)

3. The Practices of Believers in Christ (Ephesians 4:1-32)

4. The Authority of the Believer in Christ (Ephesians 5:1-6:24)

WHAT IS SALVATION?

"For by grace you have been saved through faith, and that not of yourselves; it is the gift of God." Ephesians 2:8

Scripture tells us that we are saved from a life of sin and delivered from the power of death only through faith in the resurrected Lord, Jesus Christ. Jesus proclaimed that He – and He alone – is "the Way, the Truth, and the Life. No one comes to the Father except through Me" (John 14:6). If you have never prayed a Prayer of Salvation before, we encourage you to do this today:

A Salvation Prayer

"Jesus – I come to You today as a sinner who needs salvation. I repent of my sins and I believe that You died for my sins. I ask You for forgiveness. I confess You as my Lord and I believe in my heart God raised you from the dead. I surrender my life to You completely. Thank You for loving me, forgiving me, and giving me eternal life. In Jesus Name, Amen."

WELCOME TO THE FAMILY!

Friend, we're thrilled you've accepted Jesus as your Lord and Savior. You've been born again (John 3:3-8) and adopted into God's family (Ephesians 1:5). Here are a few next steps you can take this week to keep growing in your walk with Jesus:

Water Baptism: Publicly declare your faith by getting baptized (Matthew 28:19; Luke 3:1-22).

- **Try this:** Contact a local church and invite family/friends.

Daily Devotion: Build your relationship with God through Bible reading and prayer.

- **Try this:** Get a Bible and journal; use the P.R.A.Y. method to start.

Faithful Fellowship & Serving: Join a church for support, worship, and opportunities to serve others (Matthew 20:28; Acts 2:42-47; Hebrews 10:24-25).

- **Try this:** Visit a church this weekend; pray for guidance and begin serving others as Christ served people.

Remember - you're not alone—God promises to never leave you (Hebrews 13:5; Matthew 28:20). Keep growing, praying and trusting Him day by day. If you have questions, reach out to a trusted pastor or believer. We're cheering you on in your new life in Christ!

Date _____ / _____ / _________

PREVIEW QUESTIONS

1. What do I hope goes well in my discipleship journey with Jesus this week?

....

....

....

....

....

2. What are some steps I can take this week that will help me grow in greater intimacy with Jesus?

....

....

....

....

....

3. What are some ways I can remain open and attentive to the guidance of the Holy Spirit this week?

....

....

....

....

....

4. Who is someone I can share what I'm learning from God's Word with this week?

....

....

....

....

PART 1 THEME

The Authority of Christ's Position

PART 1 READINGS

Ephesians 1:1-2:10

     Date _____ / _____ / _________

PRAY

We recommend praying before reading each day. Feel free to use The Lord's Prayer (Matthew 6:9-13), The Posture Prayer (from p. 7), or your own heartfelt prayer to the Lord. You may also want to consider using one of the following "Listening Prayers" based on today's reading:

Day 1 Prayer Based on Ephesians 1:1-6

1. Lord, thank You for choosing me to be adopted into Your family in love—how wonderful You are!

2. Lord, today I confess and agree with Your word: I am chosen in Christ before the world began.

3. Father, is there anything distracting me or distancing me from You right now? If so, please show me. (Pause and listen)

4. Now, Lord, as I begin reading this passage from Ephesians, please soften my heart and open my eyes to Your Word.

Date _____ / _____ / _________

READ

Chosen Before Time
Ephesians 1 (verses 1-6)

1

Paul, an apostle of Christ Jesus through the will of God, to the saints who are at Ephesus, and the faithful in Christ Jesus: ² Grace to you and peace from God our Father and the Lord Jesus Christ.

³ Blessed be the God and Father of our Lord Jesus Christ, who has blessed us with every spiritual blessing in the heavenly places in Christ, ⁴ even as he chose us in him before the foundation of the world, that we would be holy and without defect before him in love, ⁵ having predestined us for adoption as children through Jesus Christ to himself, according to the good pleasure of his desire, ⁶ to the praise of the glory of his grace, by which he freely gave us favor in the Beloved.

ASK

Reflection / Discussion Questions

1. Behold: The Apostle Paul begins this letter to the Ephesians by giving "all praise to God." Then he lists some reasons he is so thankful to God including God choosing us, adopting us, and blessing us in Christ. Take a moment, pause, and just thank the Lord for one or more of these truths that you have received by faith as a follower of Christ.

....

....

....

....

....

....

2. Believe: In a world that often tells us our "value" and identity is based in our status, achievements and performance, this passage proclaims God has already chosen us, adopted us and blessed us with every spiritual blessing in Christ even before the world began. Are there areas of your life where you find yourself striving for acceptance and validity based on your own efforts? If so, list some of those areas and submit them to Christ – believing you've already received them:

....

....

....

....

....

....

3. Become: God's grace and adoption aren't just personal gifts: they also are intended to be expressed in community with other believers. Pick one relationship in your life today (family/friend/co-worker/church member) who could use some encouragement and reach out to them with this truth. How will you communicate with them (text/call/email/in-person chat)?

....

....

....

....

....

....

Date _____ / _____ / ________

YIELD

Take time to ask Jesus for ways that you can better obey Him today based on what you've read. Pause and take time to listen to what He may be speaking to you. Feel free to take notes below:

Now, take time to pray for the needs of others – that they may encounter the love of Jesus today.

Date _____ / _____ / _________

PRAY

We recommend praying before reading each day. Feel free to use The Lord's Prayer (Matthew 6:9-13), The Posture Prayer (from p. 7), or your own heartfelt prayer to the Lord. You may also want to consider using one of the following "Listening Prayers" based on today's reading:

Day 2 Prayer Based on Ephesians 1:7-10

1. Lord, thank You for choosing me and redeeming me through the richness of your grace!

2. Lord, today I confess and agree with Your word: I have forgiveness in Christ for my sins.

3. Father, is there anything distracting me or distancing me from You right now? If so, please show me. (Pause and listen)

4. Now, Lord, as I begin reading this passage from Ephesians, please soften my heart and open my eyes to Your Word.

Date _____ / _____ / _________

READ

Redeemed, Forgiven, and Rich in Grace
Ephesians 1 (verses 7-10)

1

[7] In him we have our redemption through his blood, the forgiveness of our trespasses, according to the riches of his grace [8] which he made to abound toward us in all wisdom and prudence, [9] making known to us the mystery of his will, according to his good pleasure which he purposed in him [10] to an administration of the fullness of the times, to sum up all things in Christ, the things in the heavens and the things on the earth, in him.

ASK

Reflection / Discussion Questions

1. Behold: Paul continues his praise - thanking God for redemption through Christ's blood – the forgiveness of sin. Take a moment and personally thank God for Christ's blood forgiving your own sins, the riches of His grace given to you freely, and His sovereign plan to eventually bring everything together under Jesus.

....

....

....

....

....

....

2. Believe: The world often reminds us of our mistakes, failures, and short-comings resulting in guilt and shame. This passage, however, points to God forgiving our sins based on what Christ did for us on the Cross according to the richness of His grace. Are there areas of your life where you wrestle with any guilt or shame from the past; making you feel unworthy or unforgiven by God? If so, express that to the Lord, and believe in your heart that Christ's blood is sufficient to forgive you today.

....

....

....

....

....

....

3. Become: Do you know someone else who may be struggling with areas of guilt or shame today? If so, what are some ways that you could pray for them and encourage them with the truth of God's word from this passage of Ephesians?

....

....

....

....

....

....

Date _____ / _____ / _________

YIELD

Take time to ask Jesus for ways that you can better obey Him today based on what you've read. Pause and take time to listen to what He may be speaking to you. Feel free to take notes below:

Now, take time to pray for the needs of others – that they may encounter the love of Jesus today.

Date _______ / _______ / _________

PRAY

We recommend praying before reading each day. Feel free to use The Lord's Prayer (Matthew 6:9-13), The Posture Prayer (from p. 7), or your own heartfelt prayer to the Lord. You may also want to consider using one of the following "Listening Prayers."

Day 3 Prayer Based on Ephesians 1:11-14

1. Father, thank You for the wonderful blessings You've given to me by your grace!

2. Lord, today I confess and agree with Your word: I am sealed with Your Holy Spirit as a guarantee of my inheritance.

3. Father, is there anything distracting me or distancing me from You right now? If so, please show me. (Pause and listen)

4. Now, Lord, as I begin reading this passage from Ephesians, please soften my heart and open my eyes to Your Word.

Date _____ / _____ / _________

READ

Sealed with a Promise
Ephesians 1 (verses 11-14)

1

[11] We were also assigned an inheritance in him, having been foreordained according to the purpose of him who does all things after the counsel of his will, [12] to the end that we should be to the praise of his glory, we who had before hoped in Christ.

[13] In him you also, having heard the word of the truth, the Good News of your salvation—in whom, having also believed, you were sealed with the promised Holy Spirit, [14] who is a pledge of our inheritance, to the redemption of God's own possession, to the praise of his glory.

                    Date _____ / _____ / ________

ASK

Reflection / Discussion Questions

1. Behold: Paul continues encouraging praise this time for the fact that God made us His inheritance for the praise of His glory. God planned this long ago according to His perfect will. He even states that believers are "sealed with a promise." How does this make you feel about God's love, provision, and care for you today?

....

....

....

....

....

....

2. Believe: Often the world makes us feel like we're totally on our own – like we have to earn it, prove it, and secure it all by ourself. This passage shouts at us that we are already God's chosen treasure who has been sealed by His Spirit and guaranteed an inheritance in Christ. Is there an area of your life where you feel the need to strive, hustle, or take shortcuts in order to earn your acceptance in Christ or in life? If so, how can you grow in believing that this passage is for you and your life today?

....

....

....

....

....

....

3. Become: The same Holy Spirit who seals you and is in you also wants to flow through you into the lives of others. Who do you know that sometimes struggles with feeling unaccepted, unknown, or hopeless about their future that could use some encouragement from this passage in Ephesians today?

....

....

....

....

....

Date _____ / _____ / ________

YIELD

Take time to ask Jesus for ways that you can better obey Him today based on what you've read. Pause and take time to listen to what He may be speaking to you. Feel free to take notes below:

....

....

....

....

....

....

....

....

....

....

Now, take time to pray for the needs of others – that they may encounter the love of Jesus today.

....

....

....

....

....

....

....

....

....

Date _______ / _______ / ___________

PRAY

We recommend praying before reading each day. Feel free to use The Lord's Prayer (Matthew 6:9-13), The Posture Prayer (from p. 7), or your own heartfelt prayer to the Lord. You may also want to consider using one of the following "Listening Prayers" based on today's reading:

Day 4 Prayer Based on Ephesians 1:15-18

1. Father, I want to just pause and say thank You for all of the incredible people who have prayed for me over the years!

2. Lord, today I confess and agree with Your word: The eyes of my understanding are being opened to Your truth by Your grace and love for me in Christ Jesus.

3. Father, is there anything distracting me or distancing me from You right now? If so, please show me. (Pause and listen)

4. Now, Lord, as I begin reading this passage from Ephesians, please soften my heart and open my eyes to Your Word.

Date _____ / _____ / _________

READ

Called into Inheritance
Ephesians 1 (verses 15-18)

1

[15] For this cause I also, having heard of the faith in the Lord Jesus which is among you and the love which you have toward all the saints, [16] don't cease to give thanks for you, making mention of you in my prayers, [17] that the God of our Lord Jesus Christ, the Father of glory, may give to you a spirit of wisdom and revelation in the knowledge of him, [18] having the eyes of your hearts enlightened, that you may know what is the hope of his calling, and what are the riches of the glory of his inheritance in the saints.

ASK

Reflection / Discussion Questions

1. Behold: Paul says that based on the faith and love he has heard about from the believers in Ephesians, he consistently gives thanks to God and prays God's strength and wisdom for them. Who are some people in your life that inspire your faith? Take a moment and praise God for the blessing they are to you.

....

....

....

....

....

....

2. Believe: We chase for knowledge everywhere: internet news sites, podcasts, self-help books and social media posts. Here Paul prays that people will have the "eyes of their hearts enlightened" to real hope, wisdom and acceptance in Christ. Where are you still "foggy" about your calling in life or the inheritance you have as a member of the body of Christ? How can you bring those areas of uncertainty to the certainty of God's promises for you today?

....

....

....

....

....

....

3. Become: Our faith is essentially "personal" but it isn't supposed to be exclusively "private." Who is someone in your circle of life that you feel needs to have the "eyes of their understanding enlightened" to the plans and purpose God has for them? How can you connect with them and share with them this good news?

....

....

....

....

....

Date _____ / _____ / _________

YIELD

Take time to ask Jesus for ways that you can better obey Him today based on what you've read. Pause and take time to listen to what He may be speaking to you. Feel free to take notes below:

....

....

....

....

....

....

....

....

....

....

Now, take time to pray for the needs of others – that they may encounter the love of Jesus today.

....

....

....

....

....

....

....

....

....

Date _____ / _____ / ________

PRAY

We recommend praying before reading each day. Feel free to use The Lord's Prayer (Matthew 6:9-13), The Posture Prayer (from p. 7), or your own heartfelt prayer to the Lord. You may also want to consider using one of the following "Listening Prayers" based on today's reading:

Day 5 Prayer Based on Ephesians 1:19-23

1. Father, I want to thank You that all things are under Christ's feet today!

2. Lord, today I confess and agree with Your word: Because I believe in You, I have great power working in me today - the same power that raised Your Son Jesus from the dead.

3. Father, is there anything distracting me or distancing me from You right now? If so, please show me. (Pause and listen)

4. Now, Lord, as I begin reading this passage from Ephesians, please soften my heart and open my eyes to Your Word.

Date _____ / _____ / _________

READ

Christ Above All
Ephesians 1 (verses 19-23)

1

[19] and what is the exceeding greatness of his power toward us who believe, according to that working of the strength of his might [20] which he worked in Christ when he raised him from the dead and made him to sit at his right hand in the heavenly places, [21] far above all rule, authority, power, dominion, and every name that is named, not only in this age, but also in that which is to come.

[22] He put all things in subjection under his feet, and gave him to be head over all things for the assembly, [23] which is his body, the fullness of him who fills all in all.

                                    Date _____ / _____ / _________

ASK

Reflection / Discussion Questions

1. Behold: Paul proclaims that God has placed "all things in subjection under His (Christ's) feet" and that He ultimately reigns supreme over all things in Heaven and in Earth. How does that make you feel about the authority of Jesus today?

....

....

....

....

....

....

2. Believe: We can often feel overwhelmed, outsmarted, and over-matched by the world and all of its dysfunctional distractions. Is there a particular area in your life where you feel a sense of powerlessness today? If so, how can reflecting on the truth Paul shares here about Christ's resurrection power become a catalyst for you to believe in the authority you have as a believer in Christ to overcome what is trying to overwhelm you today?

....

....

....

....

....

....

3. Become: Resurrection power isn't something we are just supposed to celebrate on Easter Sunday morning. It is a reality that we should expect to experience every day as a member of the Body of Christ in which Christ is the Head. Who around you needs to know that this power is real, powerful and available to all believers today?

....

....

....

....

....

YIELD

Take time to ask Jesus for ways that you can better obey Him today based on what you've read. Pause and take time to listen to what He may be speaking to you. Feel free to take notes below:

Now, take time to pray for the needs of others – that they may encounter the love of Jesus today.

Date _______ / _______ / __________

PRAY

We recommend praying before reading each day. Feel free to use The Lord's Prayer (Matthew 6:9-13), The Posture Prayer (from p. 7), or your own heartfelt prayer to the Lord. You may also want to consider using one of the following "Listening Prayers" based on today's reading:

Day 6 Prayer Based on Ephesians 2:1-5

1. Father, I want to thank You for making me alive to Your ways and Your Word today!

2. Lord, today I confess and agree with Your word: Although I once walked in darkness, because of Your great love and mercy, I now walk in the light of Jesus Christ.

3. Father, is there anything distracting me or distancing me from You right now? If so, please show me. (Pause and listen)

4. Now, Lord, as I begin reading this passage from Ephesians, please soften my heart and open my eyes to Your Word.

Date _____ / _____ / ________

READ

Made Alive in Christ
Ephesians 2 (verses 1-5)

2

[1] You were made alive when you were dead in transgressions and sins, [2] in which you once walked according to the course of this world, according to the prince of the power of the air, the spirit who now works in the children of disobedience.

[3] We also all once lived among them in the lusts of our flesh, doing the desires of the flesh and of the mind, and were by nature children of wrath, even as the rest.

[4] But God, being rich in mercy, for his great love with which he loved us,

[5] even when we were dead through our trespasses, made us alive together with Christ—by grace you have been saved—

ASK

Reflection / Discussion Questions

1. Behold: This passage is a reminder of a reality check we need every now and again: we were once walking in darkness, pursuing a godless life, dead in our sins. But God – who is rich in mercy – made us alive with Christ by His grace. Pure grace. Pause a moment and thank God for the massive "But God" grace He has on your life that brought you into His family.

....

....

....

....

....

....

2. Believe: Sometimes we may feel like we are going back to our old ways: bad habits; anger; jealousy; pride. This passage, however, tells us a powerful truth from God's word: although we once lived that way – now we live a new way through faith in Christ. What are some areas of life where you feel like something is "dead" and not "alive" with Christ? How can you practice believing this passage is true for you today?

....

....

....

....

....

....

3. Become: What is one of your own "But God" mercy moments? Who is someone that you've shared a story of the miracle of God's grace in your life with recently? Who do you know that might be encouraged by that testimony today?

....

....

....

....

....

Date _____ / _____ / _________

YIELD

Take time to ask Jesus for ways that you can better obey Him today based on what you've read. Pause and take time to listen to what He may be speaking to you. Feel free to take notes below:

Now, take time to pray for the needs of others – that they may encounter the love of Jesus today.

  Date _____ / _____ / _________

PRAY

We recommend praying before reading each day. Feel free to use The Lord's Prayer (Matthew 6:9-13), The Posture Prayer (from p. 7), or your own heartfelt prayer to the Lord. You may also want to consider using one of the following "Listening Prayers."

Day 7 Prayer Based on Ephesians 2:6-10

1. Father, I want to thank You that spiritually I am seated with Christ in Heavenly places today!

2. Lord, today I confess and agree with Your word: I have been saved by Your grace – not by my works – and I am created in Christ to do good works for You in the earth today.

3. Father, is there anything distracting me or distancing me from You right now? If so, please show me. (Pause and listen)

4. Now, Lord, as I begin reading this passage from Ephesians, please soften my heart and open my eyes to Your Word.

Date _____ / _____ / _________

READ

Seated with Christ
Ephesians 2 (verses 6-10)

2

[6] and raised us up with him, and made us to sit with him in the heavenly places in Christ Jesus, [7] that in the ages to come he might show the exceeding riches of his grace in kindness toward us in Christ Jesus; [8] for by grace you have been saved through faith, and that not of yourselves; it is the gift of God, [9] not of works, that no one would boast.

[10] For we are his workmanship, created in Christ Jesus for good works, which God prepared before that we would walk in them.

Date _____ / _____ / _______

ASK

Reflection / Discussion Questions

1. Behold: God doesn't just save us – He "seats" us spiritually with Christ in Heavenly places. He did this – according to the Apostle Paul – to show off His grace and kindness to us. Wow! Let's take a moment and thankfully praise our Heavenly Father for saving us, seating us, and securing us in Christ.

....

....

....

....

....

....

2. Believe: We aren't saved BY our works – but we are saved FOR good works in Christ. Paul tells us works were designed by God specifically for us a very long time ago. How does this passage challenge you to receive God's grace as a free gift AND walk each day in the authority and confidence that God has gifted you and designed you to do good works for Him?

....

....

....

....

....

....

3. Become: In Christ we have received grace upon grace. Grace has been described as God's unearned favor where He does for us what we could never do for ourselves. Is there someone you know that needs to hear the incredible truths of this passage today? If so, who? What's one way you could reach out to them?

....

....

....

....

....

....

Date _____ / _____ / _________

YIELD

Take time to ask Jesus for ways that you can better obey Him today based on what you've read. Pause and take time to listen to what He may be speaking to you. Feel free to take notes below:

....

....

....

....

....

....

....

....

....

....

Now, take time to pray for the needs of others – that they may encounter the love of Jesus today.

....

....

....

....

....

....

....

....

PREVIEW QUESTIONS

1. What do I hope goes well in my discipleship journey with Jesus this week?

....

....

....

....

....

2. What are some steps I can take this week that will help me grow in greater intimacy with Jesus?

....

....

....

....

....

3. What are some ways I can remain open and attentive to the guidance of the Holy Spirit this week?

....

....

....

....

....

4. Who is someone I can share what I'm learning from God's Word with this week?

....

....

....

....

....

PART 2 THEME

The Authority of the Believer's Position

PART 2 READINGS

Ephesians 2:11-3:21

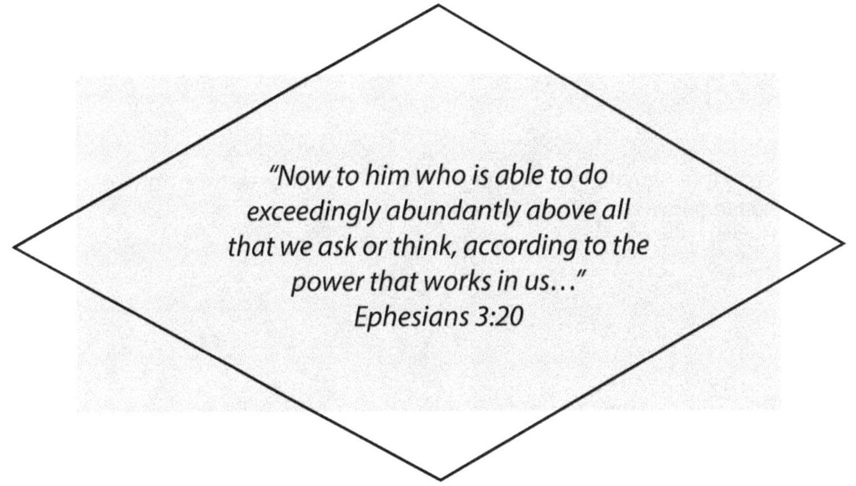

                    Date _____ / _____ / ________

PRAY

We recommend praying before reading each day. Feel free to use The Lord's Prayer (Matthew 6:9-13), The Posture Prayer (from p. 7), or your own heartfelt prayer to the Lord. You may also want to consider using one of the following "Listening Prayers."

Day 8 Prayer Based on Ephesians 2:11-13

1. Father, I want to thank You that I receive and walk in the promises of Your Covenant today!

2. Lord, today I confess and agree with Your word: Although I was once a stranger to You, You have graciously brought me near and into Your family forever through the blood of Christ.

3. Father, is there anything distracting me or distancing me from You right now? If so, please show me. (Pause and listen)

4. Now, Lord, as I begin reading this passage from Ephesians, please soften my heart and open my eyes to Your Word.

Date _____ / _____ / _________

READ

Ephesians 2 (verses 11-13)
Once Far Now Near

2

[11] Therefore remember that once you, the Gentiles in the flesh, who are called "uncircumcision" by that which is called "circumcision" (in the flesh, made by hands), [12] that you were at that time separate from Christ, alienated from the commonwealth of Israel, and strangers from the covenants of the promise, having no hope and without God in the world.

[13] But now in Christ Jesus you who once were far off are made near in the blood of Christ.

                          Date ______ / ______ / ________

ASK

Reflection / Discussion Questions

1. Behold: Paul reminds Gentiles that originally, they were once separated from God, cut off from Christ, and strangers to God's presence and His promises. Now - through the blood of Christ – Gentiles have been brought "near" to God. Pause and give God a moment of praise for the blood that bridged the gap and brought you near to Him through Christ's sacrifice.

....

....

....

....

....

....

2. Believe: We may still feel distant at times from God's presence and His promises. Like outsiders – people who don't quite "belong" to God's family – wearing labels of rejection from the past. How can you personalize the above passage in a way that helps build your faith to believe the truth: you HAVE been brought near to God through the blood of Christ.

....

....

....

....

....

....

3. Become: Being "brought near to God" is personal but it also means becoming an active member of God's family. This includes believers locally and globally. Who do you feel needs to be brought near to God today: a distant tribe half-way around the world; maybe someone living in the same house as you? How can you pray and support them in their journey of faith in Christ?

....

....

....

....

....

Date _____ / _____ / ________

YIELD

Take time to ask Jesus for ways that you can better obey Him today based on what you've read. Pause and take time to listen to what He may be speaking to you. Feel free to take notes below:

....

....

....

....

....

....

....

....

....

....

Now, take time to pray for the needs of others – that they may encounter the love of Jesus today.

....

....

....

....

....

....

....

....

....

Date _____ / _____ / _________

PRAY

We recommend praying before reading each day. Feel free to use The Lord's Prayer (Matthew 6:9-13), The Posture Prayer (from p. 7), or your own heartfelt prayer to the Lord. You may also want to consider using one of the following "Listening Prayers" based on today's reading:

Day 9 Prayer Based on Ephesians 2:14-18

1. Father, I want to thank You today for sending Jesus – The Prince of Peace – into my heart!

2. Lord, today I confess and agree with Your word: I have been reconciled to my Messianic Jewish brothers and sisters in Messiah through Christ – who broke down the wall of separation for us in His Body once and for all on the Cross.

3. Father, is there anything distracting me or distancing me from You right now? If so, please show me. (Pause and listen)

4. Now, Lord, as I begin reading this passage from Ephesians, please soften my heart and open my eyes to Your Word.

Date _____ / _____ / _________

READ

Ephesians 2 (verses 14-18)
One New Family

2

[14] For he is our peace, who made both one, and broke down the middle wall of separation, [15] having abolished in his flesh the hostility, the law of commandments contained in ordinances, that he might create in himself one new man of the two, making peace, [16] and might reconcile them both in one body to God through the cross, having killed the hostility through it.

[17] He came and preached peace to you who were far off and to those who were near [18] For through him we both have our access in one Spirit to the Father.

Date _____ / _____ / _________

ASK

Reflection / Discussion Questions

1. Behold: Jesus is our peace. He has broken down in His Body the walls that use to separate Jews and Gentiles for thousands of years and now made us One New Family in Christ. No more hostility; no more "us" versus "them." One new humanity. Let's pause and thank Jesus for allowing His body to be broken so that we could experience Shalom wholeness together today.

....

....

....

....

....

....

2. Believe: Society seeks to label and put people into categories. This often leads to comparison, division, and strife. Jesus allowed His body to be broken so that everyone who believes in Him will be saved, joined into His one family forever and experience His peace. Is there a "people group" whom you feel tension with or at odds with today? If so, ask the Lord why that is. Ask Him how you might become reconciled together in Christ.

....

....

....

....

....

....

3. Become: Paul ends this passage with a promise: through Christ, all believers have access in one Spirit to the Father. One way we can demonstrate being reconciled together with other believers is by praying together. Is there a way you could pray with other believers who may go to a different church than you? If so, what's one way you can demonstrate reconciliation in prayer?

....

....

....

....

Date _____ / _____ / _________

YIELD

Take time to ask Jesus for ways that you can better obey Him today based on what you've read. Pause and take time to listen to what He may be speaking to you. Feel free to take notes below:

....

....

....

....

....

....

....

....

....

....

Now, take time to pray for the needs of others – that they may encounter the love of Jesus today.

....

....

....

....

....

....

....

....

....

Date _____ / _____ / ________

PRAY

We recommend praying before reading each day. Feel free to use The Lord's Prayer (Matthew 6:9-13), The Posture Prayer (from p. 7), or your own heartfelt prayer to the Lord. You may also want to consider using one of the following "Listening Prayers" based on today's reading:

Day 10 Prayer Based on Ephesians 2:19-22

1. Father, I want to thank You today that I am a member of the household of faith – believers in You - both here locally and all around the world!

2. Lord, today I confess and agree with Your word: Christ is my Cornerstone, my firm foundation and I place my complete trust and confidence in Him today.

3. Father, is there anything distracting me or distancing me from You right now? If so, please show me. (Pause and listen)

4. Now, Lord, as I begin reading this passage from Ephesians, please soften my heart and open my eyes to Your Word.

Date _____ / _____ / _________

READ

Christ Our Cornerstone
Ephesians 2 (verses 19-22)

2

[19] So then you are no longer strangers and foreigners, but you are fellow citizens with the saints and of the household of God, 20 being built on the foundation of the apostles and prophets, Christ Jesus himself being the chief cornerstone; [21] in whom the whole building, fitted together, grows into a holy temple in the Lord; [22] in whom you also are built together for a habitation of God in the Spirit.

Date _____ / _____ / _________

ASK

Reflection / Discussion Questions

1. Behold: Paul proclaims something amazing here: as a believer in Christ, you are now a fully affirmed "fellow citizen with the saints and of the household of God." How does this make you feel? If you could tell God something today, what would your response be to Him for giving you the gift of this amazing title?

....

....

....

....

....

....

2. Believe: Life can be stressful and strenuous at times where we end up feeling a bit "shaky" about our circumstances, our future and/or our worth. This passage tells us Christ is our sure foundation and the "Chief Cornerstone." The cornerstone of the foundation is what everything is built upon. Are there areas of your life that feel a bit "shaky" right now (finances, health, relationships, faith)? Name one. Then say, "Jesus, I am placing this area on You – the Chief Cornerstone of my faith today."

....

....

....

....

....

....

3. Become: What God is building is not a one room studio apartment – He is building a huge temple in which all believers are being "built together into a dwelling place of God in the Spirit." Who are some faith-filled believers God's connected you to in this building process? How can you pray for them today?

....

....

....

....

....

Date _____ / _____ / _________

YIELD

Take time to ask Jesus for ways that you can better obey Him today based on what you've read. Pause and take time to listen to what He may be speaking to you. Feel free to take notes below:

....

....

....

....

....

....

....

....

....

....

Now, take time to pray for the needs of others – that they may encounter the love of Jesus today.

....

....

....

....

....

....

....

....

                    Date _____ / _____ / _________

PRAY

We recommend praying before reading each day. Feel free to use The Lord's Prayer (Matthew 6:9-13), The Posture Prayer (from p. 7), or your own heartfelt prayer to the Lord. You may also want to consider using one of the following "Listening Prayers" based on today's reading:

Day 11 Prayer Based on Ephesians 3:1-7

1. Father, I want to thank You today for Your Word and the wonderful men (like the apostle Paul) whom You used to write the Bible over thousands of years so that I can get to know You better!

2. Lord, today I confess and agree with Your word: I am a fellow-heir to all of the promises of God throughout Your Word in Christ Jesus.

3. Father, is there anything distracting me or distancing me from You right now? If so, please show me. (Pause and listen)

4. Now, Lord, as I begin reading this passage from Ephesians, please soften my heart and open my eyes to Your Word.

READ

The Mystery Revealed
Ephesians 3 (verses 1-7)

3

[1] For this cause I, Paul, am the prisoner of Christ Jesus on behalf of you Gentiles, [2] if it is so that you have heard of the administration of that grace of God which was given me toward you, [3] how that by revelation the mystery was made known to me, as I wrote before in few words, [4] by which, when you read, you can perceive my understanding in the mystery of Christ, [5] which in other generations was not made known to the children of men, as it has now been revealed to his holy apostles and prophets in the Spirit, [6] that the Gentiles are fellow heirs and fellow members of the body, and fellow partakers of his promise in Christ Jesus through the Good News, [7] of which I was made a servant according to the gift of that grace of God which was given me according to the working of his power.

ASK

Reflection / Discussion Questions

1. Behold: Paul shares about the "mystery" that has been revealed to Him by the Lord: now Gentiles have been brought into the covenant promises of God through faith in Jesus the Messiah. Pause and thank God for the blessing that this mystery is revealed: now all believers share in God's promises together!

....

....

....

....

....

....

2. Believe: Sometimes believers can battle with not believing God's promises are true for their lives – thinking they are just for other people. Do you ever feel like a second-class citizen when it comes to believing and receiving God's promises for your life? If so, what's one way you can articulate that feeling to Jesus today? Remember: He's always listening, caring, and guiding you – just like the Good Shepard of your soul.

....

....

....

....

....

....

3. Become: What are some of the promises God's word says that believers now have access to as a fellow partaker of His covenant promises? (By the way, there are several mentioned just in the first two chapters of Ephesians). Feel free to write a few of them below. How would describe these to someone else?

....

....

....

....

....

Date _____ / _____ / _________

YIELD

Take time to ask Jesus for ways that you can better obey Him today based on what you've read. Pause and take time to listen to what He may be speaking to you. Feel free to take notes below:

....

....

....

....

....

....

....

....

....

....

Now, take time to pray for the needs of others – that they may encounter the love of Jesus today.

....

....

....

....

....

....

....

....

....

Date _____ / _____ / _________

PRAY

We recommend praying before reading each day. Feel free to use The Lord's Prayer (Matthew 6:9-13), The Posture Prayer (from p. 7), or your own heartfelt prayer to the Lord. You may also want to consider using one of the following "Listening Prayers" based on today's reading:

Day 12 Prayer Based on Ephesians 3:8-10

1. Father, today I just want to pause and say thank You for your grace – the ability to do for me what I could never do for myself.

2. Lord, today I confess and agree with Your Word: You have revealed Your plan for salvation to the Church. Strengthen your Church to boldly proclaim the Gospel today!

3. Father, is there anything distracting me or distancing me from You right now? If so, please show me. (Pause and listen)

4. Now, Lord, as I begin reading this passage from Ephesians, please soften my heart and open my eyes to Your Word.

Date _____ / _____ / ________

READ

The Stewardship of the Mystery
Ephesians 3 (verses 8-10)

3

[8] To me, the very least of all saints, was this grace given, to preach to the Gentiles the unsearchable riches of Christ, [9] and to make all men see what is the administration of the mystery which for ages has been hidden in God, who created all things through Jesus Christ, [10] to the intent that now through the assembly the manifold wisdom of God might be made known to the principalities and the powers in the heavenly places.

Date _______ / _______ / _____________

ASK

Reflection / Discussion Questions

1. Behold: Paul calls himself, "the least of all saints" – yet he was chosen as a vessel by God's grace to bring good news to the Gentiles; revealing a mystery which was hidden until now. Have you ever paused and just thanked God for the wonderful news you have received by reading the Bible? Let's do that now.

....

....

....

....

....

....

2. Believe: Sometimes believers can feel "less than" or "unworthy" to do things for God. This passage states that "grace" was given to Paul so that he could carry out the wonderful task for the Lord. Is there something you feel like God has called you to do? Maybe it feels too big, too challenging, or something that you feel "unworthy" to do? If so, what role does God's grace play in helping you accomplish it?

....

....

....

....

....

....

3. Become: When Paul speaks of the "administration" of the mystery he means the faithful stewardship, management, or handling of the special project God entrusted to him. Paul was faithful in receiving the gift and he was faithful in sharing the gift. What's one way you can practice faithful stewardship to be a blessing to others by sharing with them a gift God has given you?

....

....

....

....

YIELD

Take time to ask Jesus for ways that you can better obey Him today based on what you've read. Pause and take time to listen to what He may be speaking to you. Feel free to take notes below:

Now, take time to pray for the needs of others – that they may encounter the love of Jesus today.

PRAY

We recommend praying before reading each day. Feel free to use The Lord's Prayer (Matthew 6:9-13), The Posture Prayer (from p. 7), or your own heartfelt prayer to the Lord. You may also want to consider using one of the following "Listening Prayers" based on today's reading:

Day 13 Prayer Based on Ephesians 3:11-13

1. Father, today I just want to pause and say thank You for all of the plans and purposes for humanity that You have accomplished through Your Son, Jesus Christ.

2. Lord, today I confess and agree with Your Word: I have boldness and confidence to access Your Throne of Grace through faith in Jesus Christ.

3. Holy Spirit - are there any distractions in my heart or mind that I need to lay aside today before I read?
(then pause and listen)

4. Father, is there anything distracting me or distancing me from You right now?

Date _____ / _____ / _________

READ

Confident Access by Faith
Ephesians 3 (verses 11-13)

3

[11] according to the eternal purpose which he accomplished in Christ Jesus our Lord. [12] In him we have boldness and access in confidence through our faith in him. [13] Therefore I ask that you may not lose heart at my troubles for you, which are your glory.

Date _____ / _____ / _________

ASK

Reflection / Discussion Questions

1. Behold: Through faith in Christ, now every believer has "boldness and access" to confidently come before God each day. How does it make you feel that Jesus made the way for you to have direct access to your Heavenly Father and Creator? Pause and take a moment to express to Jesus what this means for you.

....

....

....

....

....

....

2. Believe: Believers sometimes approach God timidly, or cautiously, fearing rejection, judgement, or losing heart because of life's hardships. This passage is a powerful reminder of the posture believers should have when approaching God: boldness, confidence, and assurance of access to Him through faith in Christ. Is there anything that causes you to avoid coming to God like this? If so, how can you ask Jesus to help you?

....

....

....

....

....

....

3. Become: Coming to God in faith during difficult times is hard but also some of the most rewarding times you may ever spend with Him. Likewise, praying – interceding – for someone who is grieving or distant from God is also a powerful practice. Is there anyone in your circle today whom you can spiritually - through prayer - bring confidently before God's throne of grace?

....

....

....

....

....

Date _____ / _____ / _________

YIELD

Take time to ask Jesus for ways that you can better obey Him today based on what you've read. Pause and take time to listen to what He may be speaking to you. Feel free to take notes below:

Now, take time to pray for the needs of others – that they may encounter the love of Jesus today.

Date _____ / _____ / _________

PRAY

We recommend praying before reading each day. Feel free to use The Lord's Prayer (Matthew 6:9-13), The Posture Prayer (from p. 7), or your own heartfelt prayer to the Lord. You may also want to consider using one of the following "Listening Prayers" based on today's reading:

Day 14 Prayer Based on Ephesians 3:14-19

1. Father, thank You for strengthening me today with might through Your Holy Spirit!

2. Lord, today I confess and agree with Your Word: Christ dwells in my heart through faith and I am rooted in His love.

3. Father, is there anything distracting me or distancing me from You right now? If so, please show me. (Pause and listen)

4. Now, Lord, as I begin reading this passage from Ephesians, please soften my heart and open my eyes to Your Word.

Date _____ / _____ / _________

READ

Rooted in Love

Ephesians 3 (verses 14-19)

3

14 For this cause, I bow my knees to the Father of our Lord Jesus Christ, 15 from whom every family in heaven and on earth is named, 16 that he would grant you, according to the riches of his glory, that you may be strengthened with power through his Spirit in the inner person, 17 that Christ may dwell in your hearts through faith, to the end that you, being rooted and grounded in love, 18 may be strengthened to comprehend with all the saints what is the width and length and height and depth, 19 and to know Christ's love which surpasses knowledge, that you may be filled with all the fullness of God.

Date _____ / _____ / _________

ASK

Reflection / Discussion Questions

1.Behold: This is one of the most popular and powerful prayers in the entire Bible. How can you make this prayer personalized and a prayer of thanksgiving to God? For example, "Father God, I thank You today that I am strengthened by the Holy Spirit with power in my innermost being…"

....

....

....

....

....

....

2. Believe: Paul prays that believers will have Christ dwelling in their hearts so that they are "rooted and grounded in love." Picture the condition of the soil of your heart today: is it soft with the love of Christ or is it hard; thorny; or shallow? Pick one word. List some reasons why. Then, bring your heart before Christ honestly - ask Him to soften it, deepen it, and break up whatever is keeping it from being completely filled with His love today.

....

....

....

....

....

....

3. Become: Being rooted and grounded in love is not just for us to experience God's love – it's also for us to express God's love. Jesus said that others will know that we are His disciples "if we have love for one another" (John 13:35). Ask God today who needs His love? What are 1-2 ways you can express God's love simply to them (a thoughtful text; letter; card; or phone call)?

....

....

....

....

....

Date _____ / _____ / _________

YIELD

Take time to ask Jesus for ways that you can better obey Him today based on what you've read. Pause and take time to listen to what He may be speaking to you. Feel free to take notes below:

....

....

....

....

....

....

....

....

....

....

Now, take time to pray for the needs of others – that they may encounter the love of Jesus today.

....

....

....

....

....

....

....

....

Date _______ / _______ / _________

PRAY

We recommend praying before reading each day. Feel free to use The Lord's Prayer (Matthew 6:9-13), The Posture Prayer (from p. 7), or your own heartfelt prayer to the Lord. You may also want to consider using one of the following "Listening Prayers" based on today's reading:

Day 15 Prayer Based on Ephesians 3:20-21

1. Father, thank You that You are able to do exceedingly above all that I could ever hope or think of today!

2. Lord, today I confess and agree with Your Word: I have great power working in me – the resurrection power of Christ - that gives me the ability to ask You and trust You for great things to be done for my good and for Your glory.

3. Father, is there anything distracting me or distancing me from You right now? If so, please show me. (Pause and listen)

4. Now, Lord, as I begin reading this passage from Ephesians, please soften my heart and open my eyes to Your Word.

Date _____ / _____ / ________

READ

The Power of Christ in Us

Ephesians 3 (verses 20-21)

3

[20] Now to him who is able to do exceedingly abundantly above all that we ask or think, according to the power that works in us, [21] to him be the glory in the assembly and in Christ Jesus to all generations, forever and ever. Amen.

Date _____ / _____ / _________

ASK

Reflection / Discussion Questions

1. Behold: Paul finishes this section with a heartfelt doxology of praising God for His ability to do "exceedingly above" all that we could ever ask Him to do or even think to ask Him to do! Paul prays that God's limitless ability would intersect with His perpetual power inside every believer. Tap into that power within you to give God praise for His goodness, mercy and love today.

....

....

....

....

....

....

2. Believe: Paul prays that believers will experience the God who has no limits. Do you ever find yourself limiting God? If so, name a time you felt like you prayed, believed or dreamed "too small?" Next, what do you think would happen if you began to really believe that God wanted to do "exceedingly above" all you could ever ask, think, or imagine that He would do for you?

....

....

....

....

....

....

3. Become: God's power working in us isn't just a personal fireworks show. His power in us empowers us to be witnesses for Him (see Acts 1:8). When we experience God's power, we more boldly proclaim the Gospel to others without fear. Reflect on what God's done for you and in you. Who can you share those blessings with; tapping into the power that "works within us?"

....

....

....

....

Date _____ / _____ / _________

YIELD

Take time to ask Jesus for ways that you can better obey Him today based on what you've read. Pause and take time to listen to what He may be speaking to you. Feel free to take notes below:

....

....

....

....

....

....

....

....

....

....

Now, take time to pray for the needs of others – that they may encounter the love of Jesus today.

....

....

....

....

....

....

....

....

Date _____ / _____ / _________

PREVIEW QUESTIONS

1. What do I hope goes well in my discipleship journey with Jesus this week?

....

....

....

....

....

2. What are some steps I can take this week that will help me grow in greater intimacy with Jesus?

....

....

....

....

....

3. What are some ways I can remain open and attentive to the guidance of the Holy Spirit this week?

....

....

....

....

....

4. Who is someone I can share what I'm learning from God's Word with this week?

....

....

....

....

PART 3 THEME

The Practices of Believers in Christ

PART 3 READINGS

Ephesians 4:1-32

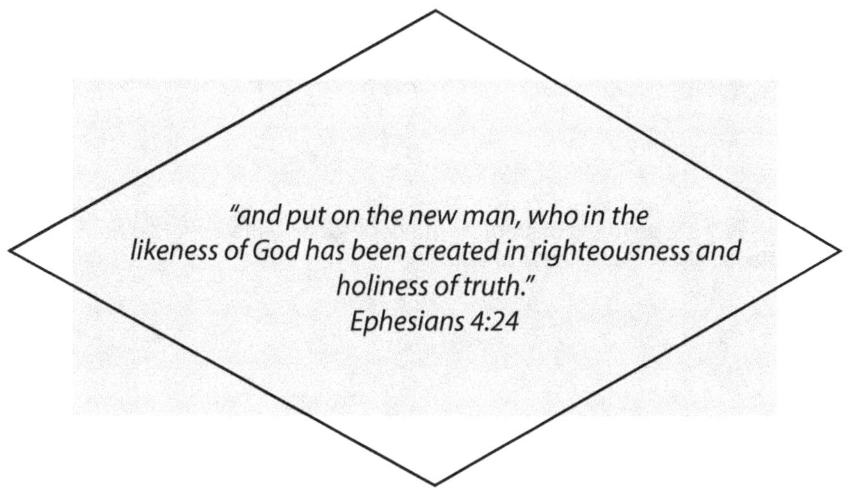

Date _____ / _____ / _________

PRAY

We recommend praying before reading each day. Feel free to use The Lord's Prayer (Matthew 6:9-13), The Posture Prayer (from p. 7), or your own heartfelt prayer to the Lord. You may also want to consider using one of the following "Listening Prayers" based on today's reading:

Day 16 Prayer Based on Ephesians 4:1-6

1. Father, thank You that there is nothing and no one better than You today!

2. Lord, today I confess and agree with Your Word: By Your grace and strength, I will walk worthy of the calling of Christ in unity and peace with others today.

3. Father, is there anything distracting me or distancing me from You right now? If so, please show me. (Pause and listen)

4. Now, Lord, as I begin reading this passage from Ephesians, please soften my heart and open my eyes to Your Word.

Date _____ / _____ / _________

READ

Walks Worthy Together
Ephesians 4 (verses 1-6)

4

[1] I therefore, the prisoner in the Lord, beg you to walk worthily of the calling with which you were called, [2] with all lowliness and humility, with patience, bearing with one another in love, [3] being eager to keep the unity of the Spirit in the bond of peace.

[4] There is one body and one Spirit, even as you also were called in one hope of your calling, [5] one Lord, one faith, one baptism, [6] one God and Father of all, who is over all and through all and in us all.

Date _____ / _____ / _________

ASK

Reflection / Discussion Questions

1. Behold: Paul's letter to the Ephesians beginning in Chapter 4 takes on a new approach: shifting from highlighting Christ's positional authority to the believer's practices in community. He starts by encouraging believers to "walk worthy" in unity – because there is only one Spirit, body, hope, Lord, faith, baptism, and God. This is the foundation of one united family in Christ. Take a moment to pray and reconcile yourself to Him today.

....

....

....

....

....

....

2. Believe: Did you realize Paul wrote this letter while he was chained as a criminal in a prison cell? Despite that, Paul urges believers to "walk worthy" in humility and patience with others. How does Paul's posture of humility during a hard season of life inspire or challenge you today?

....

....

....

....

....

....

3. Become: God's power working in us supplies us with strength to walk in unity with others – even when it's hard. Here are some of the character-building practices of unity Paul lists in this passage: meekness, patience, humility, long-suffering. Choose one of these and list one person whom you can apply it with.

....

....

....

....

....

YIELD

Take time to ask Jesus for ways that you can better obey Him today based on what you've read. Pause and take time to listen to what He may be speaking to you. Feel free to take notes below:

Now, take time to pray for the needs of others – that they may encounter the love of Jesus today.

PRAY

We recommend praying before reading each day. Feel free to use The Lord's Prayer (Matthew 6:9-13), The Posture Prayer (from p. 7), or your own heartfelt prayer to the Lord. You may also want to consider using one of the following "Listening Prayers" based on today's reading:

Day 17 Prayer Based on Ephesians 4:7-10

1. Father, thank You that You are sovereign and rule and reign above everything else today!

2. Lord, today I confess and agree with Your Word: through the generosity of Christ, I have been given a special gift in grace to serve You and others today.

3. Father, is there anything distracting me or distancing me from You right now? If so, please show me. (Pause and listen)

4. Now, Lord, as I begin reading this passage from Ephesians, please soften my heart and open my eyes to Your Word.

READ

Gifted by Grace
Ephesians 4 (verses 7-10)

4

7 But to each one of us, the grace was given according to the measure of the gift of Christ.

8 Therefore he says,

"When he ascended on high,

he led captivity captive,

and gave gifts to people."

9 Now this, "He ascended", what is it but that he also first descended into the lower parts of the earth?

10 He who descended is the one who also ascended far above all the heavens, that he might fill all things.

Date _____ / _____ / _________

ASK

Reflection / Discussion Questions

1. Behold: Paul takes his readers on a journey to help them see the source of their strength and authority as a believer to now "walk worthy" comes from the victory Christ won on the Cross and what He accomplished immediately afterwards. Re-read that passage again and take a moment to thank Jesus for His victory. Let it inspire you with strength to live for Christ today!

....

....

....

....

....

....

2. Believe: Paul reminds believers that through Christ's victory God has given grace to each including "gifts to humanity." He quotes from Psalm 68:18 and relates it to God receiving the spoils of victory and now showering gifts upon the Church. How is grace like a gift? What are some areas of your life where you feel "gifted by grace" today?

....

....

....

....

....

....

3. Become: Gifts are not supposed to be hidden in shiny boxes that get thrown into a closet unopened. Gifts are intended to be unwrapped, experienced, and enjoyed in everyday life. What are some practical ways you can use some of the unique giftings God has blessed you with to bless, encourage, or inspire someone else this week?

....

....

....

....

....

Date ____ / ____ / _______

YIELD

Take time to ask Jesus for ways that you can better obey Him today based on what you've read. Pause and take time to listen to what He may be speaking to you. Feel free to take notes below:

Now, take time to pray for the needs of others – that they may encounter the love of Jesus today.

PRAY

We recommend praying before reading each day. Feel free to use The Lord's Prayer (Matthew 6:9-13), The Posture Prayer (from p. 7), or your own heartfelt prayer to the Lord. You may also want to consider using one of the following "Listening Prayers" based on today's reading:

Day 18 Prayer Based on Ephesians 4:11-13

1. Father, I want to pause and say thank You for all the men and women serving in the Church to advance Your Gospel into the world. Bless them abundantly today I pray!

2. Lord, today I confess and agree with Your Word: I am uniquely gifted and equipped to minister and build up the Body of Christ – Your Church. Use me as a vessel of Your grace today.

3. Father, is there anything distracting me or distancing me from You right now? If so, please show me. (Pause and listen)

4. Now, Lord, as I begin reading this passage from Ephesians, please soften my heart and open my eyes to Your Word.

READ

Equipped for Ministry

Ephesians 4 (verses 11-13)

4

[11] He gave some to be apostles; and some, prophets; and some, evangelists; and some, shepherds and teachers; [12] for the perfecting of the saints, to the work of serving, to the building up of the body of Christ, [13] until we all attain to the unity of the faith and of the knowledge of the Son of God, to a full grown man, to the measure of the stature of the fullness of Christ.

Date _____ / _____ / _________

ASK

Reflection / Discussion Questions

1. Behold: Paul begins to specify some of the unique roles God has gifted people with. These roles are for advancing God's work in the world through the Church. Who do you know that walks in one of these roles today? Pause and thank God for gifting them to do what they are called to do, pray for their strength, and praise Him for blessing us with them today.

....

....

....

....

....

....

2. Believe: Paul states that these roles all work together for one purpose: to "equip" every believer to do the real work of ministry so that the Body of Christ may be built up. It's interesting that the Greek New Testament word for "ministry" is the same root word as "serve." What's one way you have been "equipped to serve" others this season and how is that making the church stronger?

....

....

....

....

....

....

3. Become: Equipping believers to serve others through an area of ministry is a strategy God gives the Church so everyone can continue to "walk worthy" as they roll up their sleeves together to help the church grow stronger and more mature. Who are some believers you know that aren't serving in an area of ministry this season? What's one way you can inspire them to join in the fun?

....

....

....

....

Date _____ / _____ / _________

YIELD

Take time to ask Jesus for ways that you can better obey Him today based on what you've read. Pause and take time to listen to what He may be speaking to you. Feel free to take notes below:

....

....

....

....

....

....

....

....

....

....

Now, take time to pray for the needs of others – that they may encounter the love of Jesus today.

....

....

....

....

....

....

....

....

....

PRAY

We recommend praying before Posture Prayer (from p. 7), or your own heartfelt prayer to the Lord. You may also want to consider using one of the following "Listening Prayers" based on today's reading:

Day 19 Prayer Based on Ephesians 4:14-16

1. Father, I want to thank You for being my Heavenly Father today who patiently guides me and provides for me like a child growing stronger in their faith in You.

2. Lord, today I confess and agree with Your Word: I am mature and grounded in Your Word. I am no longer swayed by deceptive lies – I speak the truth in love whenever called upon.

3. Father, is there anything distracting me or distancing me from You right now? If so, please show me. (Pause and listen)

4. Now, Lord, as I begin reading this passage from Ephesians, please soften my heart and open my eyes to Your Word.

READ

Builds Up the Body in Love
Ephesians 4 (verses 14-16)

4

[14] that we may no longer be children, tossed back and forth and carried about with every wind of doctrine, by the trickery of men, in craftiness, after the wiles of error; [15] but speaking truth in love, we may grow up in all things into him who is the head, Christ, [16] from whom all the body, being fitted and knit together through that which every joint supplies, according to the working in measure of each individual part, makes the body increase to the building up of itself in love.

                    Date _____ / _____ / _________

ASK

Reflection / Discussion Questions

1. Behold: While Jesus encouraged believers to be "child-like" in heart (Matthew 18:3), Paul reminds believers to not be "childish" in their walk. Believers are called to be "rooted in love." Take time to ask the Lord today how "rooted" you are in Christ's love, God's Word, and the leadership of the Holy Spirit in your life today.

....

....

....

....

....

....

2. Believe: Are there any areas in your life – or in your identity – where you feel pressured to perform, to fit in, or forced to become something just to impress others? Peer pressure is real and affects people from all walks of life. How can you bring those concerns to Jesus today? Believe with all of your heart that He loves you, cares for you and created – literally designed you - to do good works for Him (Ephesians 2:10).

....

....

....

....

....

....

3. Become: Paul also encourages believers to "speak the truth in love." He is encouraging believers who are rooted in love to speak the truth that will provide guidance to those around them. Is it possible to "speak the truth" but not "in love" to someone? If so, what's a better way you can put Pauls' words into practical action the next time an opportunity arises?

....

....

....

....

....

YIELD

Take time to ask Jesus for ways that you can better obey Him today based on what you've read. Pause and take time to listen to what He may be speaking to you. Feel free to take notes below:

....

....

....

....

....

....

....

....

....

....

Now, take time to pray for the needs of others – that they may encounter the love of Jesus today.

....

....

....

....

....

....

....

....

Date ____ / ____ / _______

PRAY

We recommend praying before reading each day. Feel free to use The Lord's Prayer (Matthew 6:9-13), The Posture Prayer (from p. 7), or your own heartfelt prayer to the Lord. You may also want to consider using one of the following "Listening Prayers" based on today's reading:

Day 20 Prayer Based on Ephesians 4:17-24

1. Father, I want to thank You for saving me and making me a New Creation with new desires and new attitudes in Christ Jesus.

2. Lord, today I confess and agree with Your Word: In Christ I throw off the old self – with its lustful desires – and I put on the new self – created to be like Christ – in light and truth.

3. Father, is there anything distracting me or distancing me from You right now? If so, please show me. (Pause and listen)

4. Now, Lord, as I begin reading this passage from Ephesians, please soften my heart and open my eyes to Your Word.

Date _____ / _____ / _________

READ

Puts off the Old; Puts on the New
Ephesians 4 (verses 17-24)

4

[17] This I say therefore, and testify in the Lord, that you no longer walk as the rest of the Gentiles also walk, in the futility of their mind, [18] being darkened in their understanding, alienated from the life of God because of the ignorance that is in them, because of the hardening of their hearts.

[19] They, having become callous, gave themselves up to lust, to work all uncleanness with greediness.

[20] But you didn't learn Christ that way, [21] if indeed you heard him and were taught in him, even as truth is in Jesus: [22] that you put away, as concerning your former way of life, the old man that grows corrupt after the lusts of deceit, [23] and that you be renewed in the spirit of your mind, [24] and put on the new man, who in the likeness of God has been created in righteousness and holiness of truth.

Date _____ / _____ / _______

ASK

Reflection / Discussion Questions

1. Behold: Re-read today's passage and use it as an opportunity to see the beautiful exchange Jesus offers us in this New Creation life. Trading old bad habits, past sins, and false assumptions for a new life rooted in Christ, renewed by the Spirit of God. Praise Him for how far He has brought you and for His faithfulness to keep you moving forward in faith today.

....

....

....

....

....

....

2. Believe: Where do you find that "old self" trying to creep in to your New Creation identity in Christ today? Are there any thoughts, words, or current actions that keep reminding you of your old self? Paul emphatically tells believers to cast those off and "learn Christ." Believe that this renewal is happening and list one or two of those areas that you can surrender to Christ today:

....

....

....

....

....

....

3. Become: Putting off the old self and putting on the new self isn't something we do as a "once and done" moment – it's a lifestyle we practice every day. Usually, the evidence of our renewed life comes in our interactions with others. Who is someone that could be blessed by the "new self" Christ is creating in you and what's one practical way you can demonstrate that with them this week (such as more patience, kindness, serving them, etc....)?

....

....

....

....

Date _______ / _______ / ___________

YIELD

Take time to ask Jesus for ways that you can better obey Him today based on what you've read. Pause and take time to listen to what He may be speaking to you. Feel free to take notes below:

Now, take time to pray for the needs of others – that they may encounter the love of Jesus today.

Date _____ / _____ / _________

PRAY

We recommend praying before reading each day. Feel free to use The Lord's Prayer (Matthew 6:9-13), The Posture Prayer (from p. 7), or your own heartfelt prayer to the Lord. You may also want to consider using one of the following "Listening Prayers" based on today's reading:

Day 21 Prayer Based on Ephesians 4:25-27

1. Father, I want to thank You for rescuing me from the power of darkness which sought to kill, steal and destroy my life. I am safe and sound in Your love and grace today, Father!

2. Lord, today I confess and agree with Your Word: In Christ, I will not give any opportunity to the devil today. I won't lie or cheat and I will not allow the sun to go down before I reconcile anything and everything that may upset me today.

3. Father, is there anything distracting me or distancing me from You right now? If so, please show me. (Pause and listen)

4. Now, Lord, as I begin reading this passage from Ephesians, please soften my heart and open my eyes to Your Word.

Date _____ / _____ / _________

READ

Gives No Opportunity for Satan

Ephesians 4 (verses 25-27)

4

[25] Therefore, putting away falsehood, speak truth each one with his neighbor, for we are members of one another.

[26] "Be angry, and don't sin."

Don't let the sun go down on your wrath, [27] and don't give place to the devil.

Date _______ / _______ / _____________

ASK

Reflection / Discussion Questions

1. Behold: Paul continues to guide us along the practices of New Testament believers and followers of Christ. He relates all believers back to their position as members of God's family and therefore we should treat each other differently. Believers must remember that in Christ, they have the power to overcome evil with good. How does that power promote praise in you today?

....

....

....

....

....

....

2. Believe: Paul quotes Psalm 4:4 and gives clarity on the topic of anger. He acknowledges that sometimes anger may be unavoidable but it will eventually open the door to sin if unresolved. Name a time you were really angry about something or with someone? How can you follow Paul's command to "not let the sun go down" before resolving it in the future?

....

....

....

....

....

....

3. Become: How could practicing the principle of not letting the "sun go down" on anger with someone help make the Gospel more attractive to them? Identify one relationship where forgiveness and reconciliation could open the door for you to share the love of Christ with them.

....

....

....

....

....

....

Date _______ / _______ / _____________

YIELD

Take time to ask Jesus for ways that you can better obey Him today based on what you've read. Pause and take time to listen to what He may be speaking to you. Feel free to take notes below:

Now, take time to pray for the needs of others – that they may encounter the love of Jesus today.

                                Date _____ / _____ / _________

PRAY

We recommend praying before reading each day. Feel free to use The Lord's Prayer (Matthew 6:9-13), The Posture Prayer (from p. 7), or your own heartfelt prayer to the Lord. You may also want to consider using one of the following "Listening Prayers" based on today's reading:

Day 22 Prayer Based on Ephesians 4:28-32

1. Father, I want to thank You that in Christ, I am sealed by the Holy Spirit for the Day of Redemption.

2. Lord, today I confess and agree with Your Word: By faith, I use my hands to work hard to be a blessing to others and I will use my words to lift others up – not tear them down. I will forgive others as Christ has forgiven me.

3. Father, is there anything distracting me or distancing me from You right now? If so, please show me. (Pause and listen)

4. Now, Lord, as I begin reading this passage from Ephesians, please soften my heart and open my eyes to Your Word.

Date _____ / _____ / _________

READ

Forgives as Christ Forgave Them
Ephesians 4 (verses 28-32)

4

28 Let him who stole steal no more; but rather let him labor, producing with his hands something that is good, that he may have something to give to him who has need.

29 Let no corrupt speech proceed out of your mouth, but only what is good for building others up as the need may be, that it may give grace to those who hear.

30 Don't grieve the Holy Spirit of God, in whom you were sealed for the day of redemption.

31 Let all bitterness, wrath, anger, outcry, and slander be put away from you, with all malice.

32 And be kind to one another, tender hearted, forgiving each other, just as God also in Christ forgave you.

                    Date _____ / _____ / _________

ASK

Reflection / Discussion Questions

1.Behold: Paul brings up a huge topic and area of need for many believers: forgiveness. He encourages believers to be kind and tender-hearted to each other and to practice "forgiving each other just as God also in Christ forgave you." Pause and thank God for forgiveness today. Let His unconditional love, mercy, and forgiveness overwhelm you so that it can overflow to others.

....

....

....

....

....

....

2. Believe: Paul gives several practical ways believers and followers of the Way of Jesus are to operate in their world: hard-working, generous, encouraging, and gracious towards others. Out of all these characteristics of a New Creation life in Christ, which ones are the most challenging for you to put into practice? Which ones are the "easiest" for you?

....

....

....

....

....

....

3. Become: "Don't grieve the Holy Spirit." Paul seems to be making the association that poor treatment of others may lead to constraining the work of the Holy Spirit in their lives. What do you think are some things that you think could "grieve," "offend," or "displease" the Holy Spirit in our relationships? How can you begin practicing the opposite of that this week with others?

....

....

....

....

....

Date _____ / _____ / _________

YIELD

Take time to ask Jesus for ways that you can better obey Him today based on what you've read. Pause and take time to listen to what He may be speaking to you. Feel free to take notes below:

....

....

....

....

....

....

....

....

....

....

Now, take time to pray for the needs of others – that they may encounter the love of Jesus today.

....

....

....

....

....

....

....

....

....

Date _____ / _____ / ________

PREVIEW QUESTIONS

1. What do I hope goes well in my discipleship journey with Jesus this week?

....

....

....

....

....

2. What are some steps I can take this week that will help me grow in greater intimacy with Jesus?

....

....

....

....

....

3. What are some ways I can remain open and attentive to the guidance of the Holy Spirit this week?

....

....

....

....

....

4. Who is someone I can share what I'm learning from God's Word with this week?

....

....

....

....

....

PART 4 THEME

The Authority of the Believer in Christ

PART 4 READINGS

Ephesians 5:1-6:24

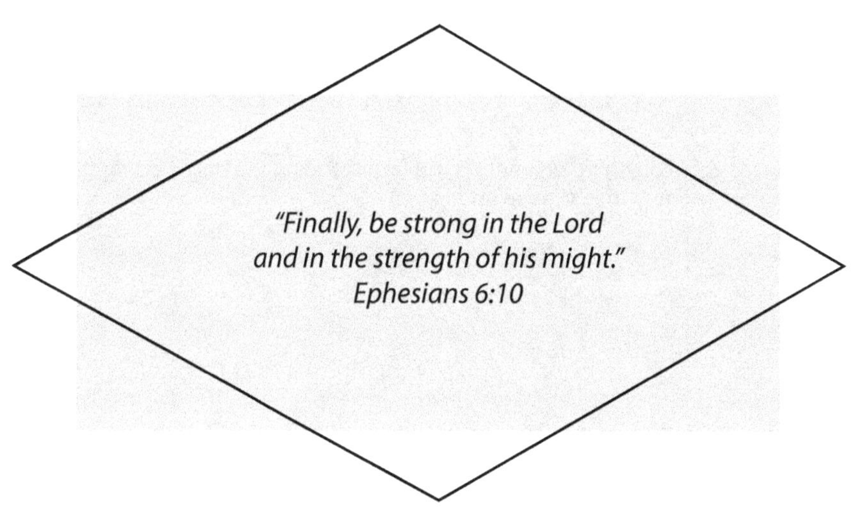

PRAY

We recommend praying before reading each day. Feel free to use The Lord's Prayer (Matthew 6:9-13), The Posture Prayer (from p. 7), or your own heartfelt prayer to the Lord. You may also want to consider using one of the following "Listening Prayers" based on today's reading:

Day 23 Prayer Based on Ephesians 5:1-7

1. Father, today I want to offer myself to You as a living sacrifice in love. Thank You for all You do me for!

2. Lord, today I confess and agree with Your Word: By Your grace, I am an imitator of Christ and renounce all immorality, impurity, and immaturity from my life. Give me Your strength to remove all that doesn't please You or resemble You today.

3. Father, is there anything distracting me or distancing me from You right now? If so, please show me. (Pause and listen)

4. Now, Lord, as I begin reading this passage from Ephesians, please soften my heart and open my eyes to Your Word.

READ

Partakers of God's Nature; Not the World's
Ephesians 5 (verses 1-7)

5

[1] Be therefore imitators of God, as beloved children.

[2] Walk in love, even as Christ also loved us and gave himself up for us, an offering and a sacrifice to God for a sweet-smelling fragrance.

[3] But sexual immorality, and all uncleanness or covetousness, let it not even be mentioned among you, as becomes saints; [4] nor filthiness, nor foolish talking, nor jesting, which are not appropriate, but rather giving of thanks.

[5] Know this for sure, that no sexually immoral person, nor unclean person, nor covetous man (who is an idolater), has any inheritance in the Kingdom of Christ and God.

[6] Let no one deceive you with empty words, for because of these things the wrath of God comes on the children of disobedience. [7] Therefore don't be partakers with them.

ASK

Reflection / Discussion Questions

1. Behold: In this final section of his letter, the Apostle Paul begins to shift his attention to the topic of family and spiritual warfare emphasizing the spiritual authority that every believer has in Christ. He first encourages believers to be "imitators of God as beloved children." Do you feel "Fathered" by God? What's a way you can embrace God as your loving Father today?

....

....

....

....

....

....

2. Believe: As a "beloved" child of God, you have been given access to tap into His divine nature – no longer imitators of the world's ways but imitators and imagers of God. What are some areas from Paul's list in this passage that resonate with you? Are there specific situations where you feel the pull to follow the worlds nature currently that you can bring to Him today?

....

....

....

....

....

....

3. Become: The power God gives us and the authority every believer has in Christ helps us protect our relationships and lead people to Him. What's one or two relationships that you feel like need "protection" today? How can you pray for them? What are some ways you can rise up in the authority of Christ and help shift their attention back to Him?

....

....

....

....

Date _____ / _____ / _________

YIELD

Take time to ask Jesus for ways that you can better obey Him today based on what you've read. Pause and take time to listen to what He may be speaking to you. Feel free to take notes below:

....

....

....

....

....

....

....

....

....

....

Now, take time to pray for the needs of others – that they may encounter the love of Jesus today.

....

....

....

....

....

....

....

....

....

Date _____ / _____ / _________

PRAY

We recommend praying before reading each day. Feel free to use The Lord's Prayer (Matthew 6:9-13), The Posture Prayer (from p. 7), or your own heartfelt prayer to the Lord. You may also want to consider using one of the following "Listening Prayers" based on today's reading:

Day 24 Prayer Based on Ephesians 5:8-14

1. Father, today I want to thank You for bringing me into Your light so I can see all that is pure, lovely, good, right and true in life!

2. Lord, today I confess and agree with Your Word: As Christ is the Light of the World, in Christ, I am a light to the world. I am awake and no longer asleep to the plans of purposes of God in my life.

3. Father, is there anything distracting me or distancing me from You right now? If so, please show me. (Pause and listen)

4. Now, Lord, as I begin reading this passage from Ephesians, please soften my heart and open my eyes to Your Word.

Date _____ / _____ / ________

READ

Living as Light

Ephesians 5 (verses 8-14)

5

[8] For you were once darkness, but are now light in the Lord. Walk as children of light, 9 for the fruit of the Spirit is in all goodness and righteousness and truth, 10 proving what is well pleasing to the Lord.

[11] Have no fellowship with the unfruitful deeds of darkness, but rather even reprove them.

[12] For it is a shame even to speak of the things which are done by them in secret.

[13] But all things, when they are reproved, are revealed by the light, for everything that reveals is light.

[14] Therefore he says, "Awake, you who sleep, and arise from the dead, and Christ will shine on you."

ASK

Reflection / Discussion Questions

1. Behold: Paul again reminds believers that positionally they are God's children and therefore should live as "children of the light." Light reflects righteous living but also means living in understanding. Those who live in darkness aren't only separated from God - they also live life with a lack of understanding. Take time to praise God today for the light He's brought into your life.

....

....

....

....

....

....

2. Believe: Think about it - nothing healthy grows in darkness. As we live our lives in right standing with God we live in the light and produce the fruit of the Spirit. Those who live in darkness produce "unfruitful works." What's an example of an area of your life where you used to hide – perhaps in shame, guilt or fear – that you now live in the light? How has God helped you with that?

....

....

....

....

....

....

3. Become: Living in the light is no longer about "blending in" it's about standing out by standing up for God, His word, and His ways of living life the right way. Illicit behavior should not be condoned in conversation – it should be an opportunity to "speak the truth in love." How can you become more of a "bright light" to your friends, co-workers, and neighbors this season?

....

....

....

....

....

Date _____ / _____ / _________

YIELD

Take time to ask Jesus for ways that you can better obey Him today based on what you've read. Pause and take time to listen to what He may be speaking to you. Feel free to take notes below:

....

....

....

....

....

....

....

....

....

....

Now, take time to pray for the needs of others – that they may encounter the love of Jesus today.

....

....

....

....

....

....

....

....

....

                    Date _____ / _____ / _______

PRAY

We recommend praying before reading each day. Feel free to use The Lord's Prayer (Matthew 6:9-13), The Posture Prayer (from p. 7), or your own heartfelt prayer to the Lord. You may also want to consider using one of the following "Listening Prayers" based on today's reading:

Day 25 Prayer Based on Ephesians 5:15-21

1. Father, today I just want to pause and give thanks to You for everything You've done and everything You are doing in Jesus Christ.

2. Lord, today I confess and agree with Your Word: In Christ I no longer waste time. I make the best of my time as a wise person who knows how valuable time is.

3. Father, is there anything distracting me or distancing me from You right now? If so, please show me. (Pause and listen)

4. Now, Lord, as I begin reading this passage from Ephesians, please soften my heart and open my eyes to Your Word.

READ

Redeeming the Time

Ephesians 5 (verses 15-21)

5

[15] Therefore watch carefully how you walk, not as unwise, but as wise, [16] redeeming the time, because the days are evil.

[17] Therefore, don't be foolish, but understand what the will of the Lord is.

[18] Don't be drunken with wine, in which is dissipation, but be filled with the Spirit, [19] speaking to one another in psalms, hymns, and spiritual songs; singing and making melody in your heart to the Lord; [20] giving thanks always concerning all things in the name of our Lord Jesus Christ to God, even the Father; [21] subjecting yourselves to one another in the fear of Christ.

Date _______ / _______ / _________

ASK

Reflection / Discussion Questions

1. Behold: Paul encourages believers to always be overflowing with praise and thanksgiving to God. "Singing and making melody in your heart to the Lord." You've had many opportunities to do this over the past month while on this journey. How does thanksgiving and praise to God affect your day? Your life?

....

....

....

....

....

....

2. Believe: Time slips by really fast! Being careless with our time by chasing distractions, foolish carousing, or selfish living can steal precious time away from us and what God intends for good. Paul encourages believers to "redeem time." What does that mean for your life this season? How can you rise up in the authority of Christ and really prove to yourself and others how valuable your time is?

....

....

....

....

....

....

3. Become: Paul encourages believers to not only be thankful to God personally – but to engage in thanksgiving and praise to God with others ("speaking to one another..."). What does it look like for you to worship and give praise to God in community this season? What are some other ways (besides musically) that you can share God's goodness with others?

....

....

....

....

.

Date _____ / _____ / _________

YIELD

Take time to ask Jesus for ways that you can better obey Him today based on what you've read. Pause and take time to listen to what He may be speaking to you. Feel free to take notes below:

....

....

....

....

....

....

....

....

....

....

Now, take time to pray for the needs of others – that they may encounter the love of Jesus today.

....

....

....

....

....

....

....

....

....

Date _____ / _____ / ________

PRAY

We recommend praying before reading each day. Feel free to use The Lord's Prayer (Matthew 6:9-13), The Posture Prayer (from p. 7), or your own heartfelt prayer to the Lord. You may also want to consider using one of the following "Listening Prayers" based on today's reading:

Day 26 Prayer Based on Ephesians 5:22-33

1. Father, today I thank You for families: My own and others - and I pray that You will bless them abundantly today.

2. Lord, today I confess and agree with Your Word: In Christ I submit to You and to one another in love. I pray that all husbands love their wives and that all wives respect their husbands today in Christ Jesus.

3. Father, is there anything distracting me or distancing me from You right now? If so, please show me. (Pause and listen)

4. Now, Lord, as I begin reading this passage from Ephesians, please soften my heart and open my eyes to Your Word.

Date _____ / _____ / _________

READ

Loving and Respectful Marriages
Ephesians 5 (verses 22-33)

5

22 Wives, be subject to your own husbands, as to the Lord. 23 For the husband is the head of the wife, as Christ also is the head of the assembly, being himself the savior of the body. 24 But as the assembly is subject to Christ, so let the wives also be to their own husbands in everything.

25 Husbands, love your wives, even as Christ also loved the assembly and gave himself up for her, 26 that he might sanctify her, having cleansed her by the washing of water with the word, 27 that he might present the assembly to himself gloriously, not having spot or wrinkle or any such thing, but that she should be holy and without defect.

28 Even so husbands also ought to love their own wives as their own bodies. He who loves his own wife loves himself. 29 For no man ever hated his own flesh, but nourishes and cherishes it, even as the Lord also does the assembly, 30 because we are members of his body, of his flesh and bones.

31 "For this cause a man will leave his father and mother and will be joined to his wife. Then the two will become one flesh." 32 This mystery is great, but I speak concerning Christ and the assembly.

33 Nevertheless each of you must also love his own wife even as himself; and let the wife see that she respects her husband.

ASK

Reflection / Discussion Questions

1. Behold: Paul turns his readers attention to the home. He paints marriage as a living picture of what Christ does for the Church. Are you currently married or know someone who is? Take time today to lift those marriages up to the Lord. Pray that God will bless them, strengthen them, and help them resemble Christ.

....

....

....

....

....

....

2. Believe: In a world that often paints marriage in a negative light of division, distrust, and disunity, Paul shows a better way. God's plan for marriage is based on mutual honor rooted in honoring Christ: wives respecting their husbands and husbands loving their wives. After reading this passage, list the characteristics of a godly marriage that's based upon Scripture. How could marriages today benefit from practicing these characteristics?

....

....

....

....

....

....

3. Become: Marriage is wonderful but rarely "easy." It's a relationship that takes a lot of strength, prayer, and support. Are there 1-2 ways you can strengthen and support marriages this season? Are there couples you could cook dinner for? Or offer to watch their kids so they could have a date night? Are any marriages "on the rocks" who need your prayers this season?

....

....

....

....

....

Date _____ / _____ / _________

YIELD

Take time to ask Jesus for ways that you can better obey Him today based on what you've read. Pause and take time to listen to what He may be speaking to you. Feel free to take notes below:

....

....

....

....

....

....

....

....

....

....

Now, take time to pray for the needs of others – that they may encounter the love of Jesus today.

....

....

....

....

....

....

....

....

....

PRAY

We recommend praying before reading each day. Feel free to use The Lord's Prayer (Matthew 6:9-13), The Posture Prayer (from p. 7), or your own heartfelt prayer to the Lord. You may also want to consider using one of the following "Listening Prayers" based on today's reading:

Day 27 Prayer Based on Ephesians 6:1-4

1. Father, today I thank You that Jesus said we all must have child-like faith in order to see Your Kingdom here on Earth. Lord I am thankful to be called Your child today!

2. Lord, today I confess and agree with Your Word: In Christ, I honor my parents as to the Lord and I pray for all children that I know of to honor their parents as well so that their lives may be blessed according to Your Word. Strengthen parents to lead them in Christlikeness today I pray in Jesus name.

3. Father, is there anything distracting me or distancing me from You right now? If so, please show me. (Pause and listen)

4. Now, Lord, as I begin reading this passage from Ephesians, please soften my heart and open my eyes to Your Word.

READ

Honoring and Nurturing Families
Ephesians 6 (verses 1-4)

6

[1] Children, obey your parents in the Lord, for this is right.

[2] "Honor your father and mother," which is the first commandment with a promise:

[3] "that it may be well with you,
and you may live long on the earth."

[4] You fathers, don't provoke your children to wrath, but nurture them in the discipline and instruction of the Lord.

Date _____ / _____ / _________

ASK

Reflection / Discussion Questions

1. Behold: Paul turns his attention from marriage to parenting. Do you have children in your home this season or know others who do? Let's pause and thank God for them and pray for the kids to honor and obey their parents in the Lord so they can be blessed and pray for peace and unity in the home.

....

....

....

....

....

....

2. Believe: Paul wants believers to know the power and authority they have in Christ for everyday life - and that includes the children. Children should be encouraged to become fully devoted followers of Jesus and learn to walk in His ways. Parenting – like marriage – is never easy but it can be wonderfully rewarding. What do you take away from Paul's encouragement to children here - quoting from Exodus 20:12?

....

....

....

....

....

....

3. Become: Paul doesn't just stop at encouraging the kids in this passage, he also has a reminder for the parents: "don't provoke" them which may cause them to harbor resentment. Instead, "nurture them" in the ways and Words of Jesus. Just like marriages, parents are under pressure these days. Are there 1-2 ways you can help serve children or parents this season?

....

....

....

....

....

....

Date _____ / _____ / _________

YIELD

Take time to ask Jesus for ways that you can better obey Him today based on what you've read. Pause and take time to listen to what He may be speaking to you. Feel free to take notes below:

Now, take time to pray for the needs of others – that they may encounter the love of Jesus today.

PRAY

We recommend praying before reading each day. Feel free to use The Lord's Prayer (Matthew 6:9-13), The Posture Prayer (from p. 7), or your own heartfelt prayer to the Lord. You may also want to consider using one of the following "Listening Prayers" based on today's reading:

Day 28 Prayer Based on Ephesians 6:5-9

1. Father, today I thank You that your word says You will reward us one day for the good we do for You on Earth. Thank You for being a rewarder of those who see to honor You in all they do.

2. Lord, today I confess and agree with Your Word: I have great power working in me today – the resurrection power of Christ - that gives me the ability to ask You and trust You for great things to be done for my good and for Your glory.

3. Father, is there anything distracting me or distancing me from You right now? If so, please show me. (Pause and listen)

4. Now, Lord, as I begin reading this passage from Ephesians, please soften my heart and open my eyes to Your Word.

READ

Worshipping While Working

Ephesians 6 (verses 5-9)

6

[5] Servants, be obedient to those who according to the flesh are your masters, with fear and trembling, in singleness of your heart, as to Christ, 6 not in the way of service only when eyes are on you, as men pleasers, but as servants of Christ, doing the will of God from the heart, [7] with good will doing service as to the Lord and not to men, [8] knowing that whatever good thing each one does, he will receive the same good again from the Lord, whether he is bound or free.

[9] You masters, do the same things to them, and give up threatening, knowing that he who is both their Master and yours is in heaven, and there is no partiality with him.

ASK

Reflection / Discussion Questions

1. Behold: Paul transitions from taking the Gospel into the home to bringing it into the workplace. Are you currently employed? If so, remember that God is your Source – your job is just a resource. Let's take a moment to thank God for the jobs we have and pray for our supervisors – that they may be strengthened, blessed, and create a godly workplace environment.

....

....

....

....

....

....

2. Believe: Paul contrasts those who work for their "master" (employers) versus those who work for the Lord while working at their job. Which category do you tend to fall into while you are working? By the way, being a homemaker entails a lot of work, so this includes them as well! What are some ways you can focus more on God being your rewarder at work this season?

....

....

....

....

....

....

3. Become: The world usually tries to separate jobs into "secular work" versus "spiritual work." However, Paul says that there is no separation - Christ is Lord of every job, every boss, and every task. Walking in our authority as believers empowers us to serve others at work with integrity, joy, and excellence. What impact could believers have at their workplaces with this mindset?

....

....

....

....

....

Date _____ / _____ / _________

YIELD

Take time to ask Jesus for ways that you can better obey Him today based on what you've read. Pause and take time to listen to what He may be speaking to you. Feel free to take notes below:

....

....

....

....

....

....

....

....

....

....

Now, take time to pray for the needs of others – that they may encounter the love of Jesus today.

....

....

....

....

....

....

....

....

....

Date _______ / _______ / __________

PRAY

We recommend praying before reading each day. Feel free to use The Lord's Prayer (Matthew 6:9-13), The Posture Prayer (from p. 7), or your own heartfelt prayer to the Lord. You may also want to consider using one of the following "Listening Prayers" based on today's reading:

Day 29 Prayer Based on Ephesians 6:10-17

1. Father, today I thank You that there is no power on Earth or in the Heavens above greater than Your power!

2. Lord, today I confess and agree with Your Word: I am a soldier for Christ! I put on the full armor of God today and resist the enemy at every turn because greater is He – You Lord - that is in me than he who is in the world.

3. Father, is there anything distracting me or distancing me from You right now? If so, please show me. (Pause and listen)

4. Now, Lord, as I begin reading this passage from Ephesians, please soften my heart and open my eyes to Your Word.

Date _____ / _____ / _________

READ

Armed for Battle

Ephesians 6 (verses 10-17)

6

[10] Finally, be strong in the Lord and in the strength of his might.

[11] Put on the whole armor of God, that you may be able to stand against the wiles of the devil.

[12] For our wrestling is not against flesh and blood, but against the principalities, against the powers, against the world's rulers of the darkness of this age, and against the spiritual forces of wickedness in the heavenly places.

[13] Therefore put on the whole armor of God, that you may be able to withstand in the evil day, and having done all, to stand.

[14] Stand therefore, having the utility belt of truth buckled around your waist, and having put on the breastplate of righteousness, [15] and having fitted your feet with the preparation of the Good News of peace, [16] above all, taking up the shield of faith, with which you will be able to quench all the fiery darts of the evil one.

[17] And take the helmet of salvation, and the sword of the Spirit, which is the word of God.

                    Date _____ / _____ / _________

ASK

Reflection / Discussion Questions

1. Behold: Paul transitions his readers to remind them that there are dark spiritual forces at work in the world and that as believers it is important to stand firm in faith daily. He describes a spiritual battle taking place daily in which believers need to resist demonic influences, put on the armor of God, and know Christ is victorious. How does this passage impact your daily prayer life?

....

....

....

....

....

....

2. Believe: The enemy wants us to try and find him on his terms and in our strength. Re-read Ephesians 6:10. Where does it say that the believer's authority, strength, and power come from? What are 3 ways you can remind yourself each day to "be strong in the LORD and the power of HIS might?" What are some ways this could play out in your life practically this week?

....

....

....

....

....

....

3. Become: The armor of God doesn't only protect the believer – it will protect whoever stands behind the believer. Have you thought about some ways you can wear the spiritual armor of God in the workplace or at school in a way that not only protects you but other innocent victims who may be getting harassed?

....

....

....

....

....

Date _____ / _____ / _________

YIELD

Take time to ask Jesus for ways that you can better obey Him today based on what you've read. Pause and take time to listen to what He may be speaking to you. Feel free to take notes below:

....

....

....

....

....

....

....

....

....

....

Now, take time to pray for the needs of others – that they may encounter the love of Jesus today.

....

....

....

....

....

....

....

....

....

PRAY

We recommend praying before reading each day. Feel free to use The Lord's Prayer (Matthew 6:9-13), The Posture Prayer (from p. 7), or your own heartfelt prayer to the Lord. You may also want to consider using one of the following "Listening Prayers" based on today's reading:

Day 30 Prayer Based on Ephesians 6:18-24

1. Father, today I thank You for this journey through Your Word. Thank You for teaching me more of who You are and who I am in Christ this season!

2. Lord, today I confess and agree with Your Word: In Christ I am prayerful, I am purposeful, and I have power to persevere through any and all challenges through faith in Jesus Christ.

3. Father, is there anything distracting me or distancing me from You right now? If so, please show me. (Pause and listen)

4. Now, Lord, as I begin reading this passage from Ephesians, please soften my heart and open my eyes to Your Word.

READ

Prayerful, Persevering, and Purposeful

Ephesians 6 (verses 18-24)

6

[18] with all prayer and requests, praying at all times in the Spirit, and being watchful to this end in all perseverance and requests for all the saints.

[19] Pray for me, that utterance may be given to me in opening my mouth, to make known with boldness the mystery of the Good News, [20] for which I am an ambassador in chains; that in it I may speak boldly, as I ought to speak.

[21] But that you also may know my affairs, how I am doing, Tychicus, the beloved brother and faithful servant in the Lord, will make known to you all things.

[22] I have sent him to you for this very purpose, that you may know our state and that he may comfort your hearts.

[23] Peace be to the brothers, and love with faith, from God the Father and the Lord Jesus Christ.

[24] Grace be with all those who love our Lord Jesus Christ with incorruptible love. Amen.

ASK

Reflection / Discussion Questions

1. Behold: As we conclude reading the book of Ephesians today, what are you most thankful for? What are some things that you can pause and praise God for that you learned by going on this journey?

....

....

....

....

....

....

2. Believe: Paul closes out his letter prayerfully and purposefully. The spirit of God gives every believer the power to persevere in every circumstance – especially in their spiritual habits. How has your personal prayer life grown over the past month? Are there some other spiritual habits beside daily prayer you would like to continue after this? How can you bring that request to Jesus today and be strong in the power of His might?

....

....

....

....

....

....

3. Become: Paul prays at the close of his letter that everyone who loves Jesus will experience His peace, grace, and incorruptible love. What are some ways you can remind yourself in the next season of these three things? What would an example of each be? Is there someone else who needs to hear about the love, grace and peace Jesus offers them today? Pray for them.

....

....

....

....

....

....

Date _____ / _____ / ________

YIELD

Take time to ask Jesus for ways that you can better obey Him today based on what you've read. Pause and take time to listen to what He may be speaking to you. Feel free to take notes below:

Now, take time to pray for the needs of others – that they may encounter the love of Jesus today.

SMALL GROUP DISCUSSION

First of all, thank you for your willingness to engage with others using the Walking with Jesus through the New Testament series Scripture Journals. Creating spaces for biblical community is essential for churches of all sizes to flourish. In Acts 2:42, we see that biblical community was formed when believers came together to study God's Word, pray, fellowship, and even break bread together. We encourage you to gather with those in your group to decide on some of the following elements of small group ministry before getting started.

MEETING FORMAT OPTIONS

After deciding on a set day, time, and frequency (weekly or bi-weekly) to meet, we suggest choosing one of the following meeting format options:

1. **4-Week Small Group Format** – In this format, the group would discuss one of the themes together during each gathering for four meetings:

Part	Theme	Scriptures
1	The Authority of Christ's Position	Ephesians 1:1-2:10
2	The Authority of the Believers Position	Ephesians 2:11-3:21
3	The Practices of Believers in Christ	Ephesians 4:1-32
4	The Authority of the Believer in Christ	Ephesians 5:1-6:24

2. **6-Week Small Group Format** – In this format, the group would have a "Meet & Greet" during the first gathering, discuss one of the themes over each of the next 4 meetings, and then conclude with a closing night which allows an opportunity for group members to share what they learned and experienced throughout the series.

Part	Theme	Scriptures
1	"Welcome" Night (Meet & Greet)	Consider using content from the "How to Get the Most Out of This Journal" page and/or the "Overview" page
2	The Authority of Christ's Position	Ephesians 1:1-2:10
3	The Authority of the Believer's Position	Ephesians 2:11-3:21
4	The Practices of Believers in Christ	Ephesians 4:1-32
5	The Authority of the Believer in Christ	Ephesians 5:1-6:24
6	"Sharing" Night (taking time to hear from the group members what they learned during the series about the Lord, the Bible, one another and/or themselves)	Consider including food on this night and having extended times of prayer together

SUGGESTED MEETING AGENDA TIMES

Decide on the amount of time each group gathering will be expected to last (60 or 90 minutes) and then consider following the suggested times for each part of the meeting below:

1. Sample 60-minute Format:

Welcome	15 minutes	Allows time for members to fellowship, catch up, and for the leaders to make any announcements before getting started.
Segue	5 minutes	A time of transition that allows for thankfulness, reflection on the readings for the meeting, and prayer.
Discussion	30 minutes	Discuss what stood out from the "Read" section of the Scripture passages that week and any answers from the "Ask" sections of the Journals that participants would like to share and/or discuss together.
Prayer	10 minutes	Taking time to pray together to meet needs listed in the "Pray" section and/or any needs that come up during the meeting.

2. Sample 90-minute Format:

Welcome	30 minutes	Allows time for members to fellowship, catch up, and for the leaders to make any announcements before getting started.
Segue	10 minutes	A time of transition that allows for thankfulness, reflection on the readings for the meeting, and prayer.
Discussion	40 minutes	Discuss what stood out from the "Read" section of the Scripture passages that week and any answers from the "Ask" sections of the Journals that participants would like to share and/or discuss together.
Prayer	10 minutes	Taking time to pray together to meet needs listed in the "Pray" section and/or any needs that come up during the meeting.

RECOMMENDED "GROUND RULES" FOR SMALL GROUPS

Small group ministry can be both deeply rewarding and extremely challenging at times. We recommend keeping the following guidelines in place to help everyone feel accepted and for the group time to function in a healthy manner.

Discretion – Create a safe place for people to share, but avoid personal attacks and gossip.

Discussion – Be a good listener first and allow everyone an opportunity to share their views.

Direction – Keep the discussion time on track by guiding the conversations to stay on topic.

Devotion – This series is all about helping people grow in their personal devotion to Jesus by engaging with Him in prayer and by studying God's Word. Do all you can to keep this idea the main theme at every group meeting.

"Instead, we will speak the truth in love, growing in every way more and more like Christ, who is the head of his body, the Church. He makes the whole body fit together perfectly. As each part does its own special work, it helps the other parts grow, so that the whole body is healthy and growing and full of love." - Ephesians 4:15-16, NLT©

FAMILY DEVOTION GUIDE

When Jesus was asked what the greatest commandment in all of Scripture is, He quoted from Deuteronomy 6:4-9. Although this passage begins with the command to personally love the Lord with all of your heart, it extends to lovingly teaching God's Word to those in your own home:

"You shall teach them diligently to your children, and shall talk of them when you sit in your house, and when you walk by the way, and when you lie down, and when you rise up." (Deut. 6:7, NKJV©)

As we personally grow in our love for the Lord and the knowledge of His Word, it is clear that the Lord wants us to also share His Word with others – especially those in our own home. While this might seem challenging at first, please don't feel intimidated about opening God's Word together with your family. You do not have to be a theologian, Bible teacher, or expert in church history to have a family devotion. Just the simple act of children seeing their parents open God's Word in their home and talking about it together does wonders in a child's heart. We encourage you to explore various ways below to experience the blessings and benefits of bringing God's Word alive in your home using this Scripture Journal.

HOW? Formal and Informal Methods

There are both formal and informal ways of sharing God's Word together as a family. While one method may work better than the other for your family in a particular season, we encourage you to be open to mixing these up from time to time as well.

Some ways to informally discuss God's Word together could include:
1. Car ride conversations
2. Personal talks
3. Bringing up a Bible passage/reflection while doing chores/tasks together
4. Texting or messaging what stood out to you from today's reading to family members in a group chat

Some ways to formally discuss God's Word together could include:
1. Specific day, time, and place each week ("Family Devotion Night," for example)
2. Daily Bible reflections and discussions as a part of a specific meal time
3. Morning and/or bedtime readings and reflections
4. Honoring the Sabbath together as a family

WHAT? Content and Flow Suggestions

Each day in this Journal provides you with helpful tools to both personally engage with the Scripture and ways to engage others. The main elements of a good Family Devotion Time should include:

- Prayer
- Scripture
- Discovery Questions
- Application Opportunities

Feel free to look back on the previous pages – "Small Group Discussion Guide" – for options in pacing and prioritizing the content.

SCRIPTURE MEMORIZATION

Each week provides you with an overall theme from the chapter that could also be turned into a Memory Verse challenge for the family. Challenge kids to memorize as much as they are able to from the Weekly Passage and feel free to shorten it or adapt it for their specific reading and comprehension level. Kids (and adults) are usually pretty competitive and love a good challenge. Having a Scripture Memory Contest each week could be a wonderful way to help them commit God's Word to memory.

FAMILY DECLARATIONS

Family Declarations can also be a great way to keep everyone engaged in Scripture and may also help shape your family identity in Christ. Select a Scripture and then work together to personalize it in a way that is inspiring to the family members. For example:

But as for me and my house, we will serve the LORD."
(Joshua 24:15b NKJV)

KEEP IT FUN!

Having a regular family devotion can be challenging at times but ultimately it is also incredibly rewarding. Do all you can to stay positive and be creative. Many wonderful Christ-centered ministries provide some excellent resources – many available for free online - that can help you to keep things fresh as well. Also, feel free to ask around in your local church what other faith-filled parents are doing to help keep their kids engaged in Scripture.

STAY ENCOURAGED

God's Word reminds us that as believers we walk by faith and not by sight (2 Cor. 5:7) and that God's Word is like seed (Luke 8:11-15). When you plant a seed, it is buried deep, and you can't always tell if it is taking root and growing or not. It takes time. Keep watering, nurturing, cultivating, and **keep planting more seed**. Over time you will see things grow:

"And let us not grow weary of doing good, for in due season we will reap, if we do not give up. So then, as we have opportunity, let us do good to everyone, and especially to those who are of the household of faith."
– Galatians 6:9-10, ESV©

Congratulations!

We sincerely hope that you have enjoyed this Scripture Journal.

For more in this series, "Walking with Jesus through the New Testament" by Dr. Bob Neal, search for these titles wherever books are sold.

For bulk orders, email us at:
info@alongtheway121.com

Visit his Amazon Author Central page to explore more: